A Note to Parents

DK READERS is a compelling program for beginning readers, designed in conjunction with leading literacy experts, including Dr. Linda Gambrell, Distinguished Professor of Education at Clemson University. Dr. Gambrell has served as President of the National Reading Conference, the College Reading Association, and the International Reading Association.

Beautiful illustrations and superb full-color photographs combine with engaging, easy-to-read stories to offer a fresh approach to each subject in the series. Each DK READER is guaranteed to capture a child's interest while developing his or her reading skills, general knowledge, and love of reading.

The five levels of DK READERS are aimed at different reading abilities, enabling you to choose the books that are exactly right for your child:

Pre-level 1: Learning to read
Level 1: Beginning to read
Level 2: Beginning to read alone
Level 3: Reading alone
Level 4: Proficient readers

The "normal" age at which a child begins to read can be anywhere from three to eight years old. Adult participation through the lower levels is very helpful for providing encouragement, discussing storylines, and sounding out unfamiliar words.

No matter which level you select, you can be sure that you are helping your child learn to read, then read to learn!

Editor Jennifer Siklós and Caroline Bingham
Designer Michelle Baxter
Senior Editor Linda Esposito
Deputy Managing Art Editor Jane Horne
US Editor Regina Kahney
Pre-Production Producer Nadine King
Producer Sara Hu
Photography Richard Leeney

Reading Consultant
Linda B. Gambrell, Ph.D.

This edition published, 2017
First American Edition, 1998
Published in the United States by DK Publishing
345 Hudson Street, New York, New York 10014

Copyright © 1998, 2017 Dorling Kindersley Limited
17 18 19 20 10 9 8 7 6 5 4 3 2
009–187993–July/1998

A catalog record for this book is available
from the Library of Congress.
ISBN: 978-1-4654-0243-1

DK books are available at special discounts when purchased
in bulk for sales promotions, premiums, fund-raising,
or educational use.
For details, contact: DK Publishing Special Markets
345 Hudson Street, New York, New York 10014

Color reproduction by Colourscan, Singapore
Printed and bound in China

The publisher would like to thank the following for their kind
permission to reproduce their photographs:
Key: t=top, b=below, l=left, r=right, c=center
Pictor International: (14-15).
Additional photography by Andy Crawford (26bl & 32 - bolt),
Ray Moller (30-31) and Alex Wilson (13t).
Cover images: Front: Dreamstime.com: Rvo233 (Background);
Back: Dreamstime.com: Volodymyrkrasyuk tl
All other images © Dorling Kindersley
For further information see: www.dkimages.com

The publisher would also like to thank
Rick Roberton at Western Truck Limited.
Special thanks to John Scholey at W Scholey & Son for the
use of his truck, time and premises.

A WORLD OF IDEAS:
SEE ALL THERE IS TO KNOW

www.dk.com

DK READERS

BEGINNING **1** TO READ

Truck Trouble

BE-16-88

Written by Angela Royston

John got up very early
to make a special delivery.
He climbed up two steps
into his big blue truck.

John looked at the map.

Today was no day to get lost!

Then he started the truck,

checked the mirrors, and set off.

mirror

At a service station,
John checked the engine.
It needed some oil.
Then he filled up the fuel tank.

fuel tank

He looked at
the shiny engine.
"Don't let me down!"
he said.
"I can't be late!"

Next he had to pick up the cargo.
A forklift raised big boxes
into the back of John's truck.

There were also some small boxes
marked "Special Delivery."
John put these in the truck too.

John was in a hurry,
but he was also
very hungry.

He pulled into a truck stop
for breakfast.

John's friend Paul arrived
in his milk tanker.
He joined John for breakfast.

But John couldn't stop for long.
He had deliveries to make!

John drove on to the freeway.

It was jammed with traffic.

Cars and trucks beeped their horns.

John had to deliver the big boxes
to a nearby factory.
He left the freeway
at the next exit.

John waved to the workers as he drove into the factory.

The workers helped him
unload the big boxes.

"I'm in a hurry,"
John told them.
"I've got another delivery
to make."
Soon he was on his way.
But there was trouble ahead.

A van had broken down!
John slammed on his brakes.
His truck screeched to a halt.

The road was very narrow.
John's truck was too wide
to get past the van.

John used his radio to call for help. He also warned all other drivers to stay away from that road.

Soon John saw flashing lights.

It was a tow truck!

The tow truck towed the van

to a garage.

When the road was clear

John hurried on his way.

But there was more trouble ahead!

Boom! Boom!

John drove into a thunderstorm.

Rain began to pour down.

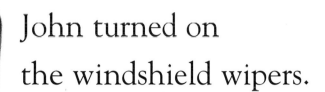

John turned on
the windshield wipers.

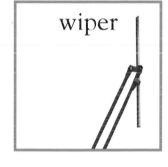

wiper

He drove very slowly.

"This isn't my day!"

he groaned.

John drove on and on.
Finally the rain stopped.
He pulled over to eat his lunch.

Then he rested on a bunk
in the back of the cab.
He fell fast asleep!

When he woke up, John thought,
"Now I'm in trouble!"

BANG!

"Oh no! A flat tire!"
John grabbed
his tools and
the spare wheel.

He unscrewed
the bolts and
took off the wheel.

bolt

Then he put on the spare.
It was hard work!

John drove into town.
He had to wait for
the traffic light
to turn green.

traffic
light

BE-16-88

"Hurry up!" thought John.
He was almost late
for his special delivery.

At last John arrived.
There was no time to spare!
He unloaded the boxes marked
"Special Delivery."

John was just in time for the party at the new children's hospital.

Inside the special boxes
were piles of toys.
"Thank you!" shouted the children.
"It was no trouble!" said John.

Glossary

Bolt
a screw without a point used to fasten things

Fuel tank
a large container for storing fuel

Mirror
a piece of glass that helps you to see what's behind you

Traffic lights
a row of red, yellow, and green lights that control traffic

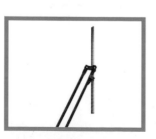

Wiper
a long thin tool that wipes away water